D1250851

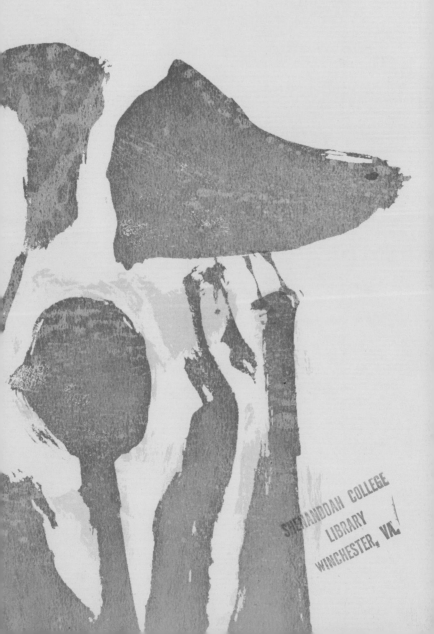

TOWER SERIES   NUMBER FOUR

Of Some Country

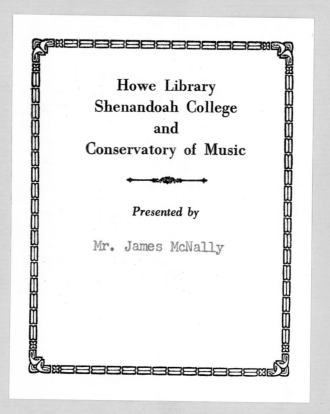

ROBERT D. FITZGERALD : *Of Some Country*

27 poems with drawings by

SISTER MARY CORITA

THE UNIVERSITY OF TEXAS

Acknowledgment is made to the Australian publishers
of the author's previous collections, to the Australian
publications *The Bulletin, Meanjin, Overland,
Southerly*, and *The Sydney Morning Herald*
and to *The Texas Quarterly*.

Library of Congress Catalogue Card Number: 63–63491

Published by THE HUMANITIES RESEARCH CENTER
THE UNIVERSITY OF TEXAS
Distributed by the UNIVERSITY OF TEXAS PRESS
AUSTIN 12, TEXAS

Printed and bound in the United States of America

CONTENTS

Favour

I'll not touch wood nor, fingers crossed,
creep furtively for fear all's lost.
Luck's liquor pounding through the brain
I'll stand on kerbs and bellow
great news at my indifferent kin—
her favour towards this fellow.

Would you treat gently with that rowdy?
Flaunt or you flout her: Luck's no lady.
Yours in the lavish minute while
you take her gifts two-handed,
she'll break your heart for you, and smile,
so soon as she's so minded.

And pick your pocket when she goes . . .
But snap time's tail up: that hour's woes
will not snake round at now, bite back
where a game grip jerks a summons—
Luck loves him longest who can crack
this kind of lash on omens.

Of Some Country

Though he has loved you and been glad,
his world re-built, his stars made new,
take note of how that fidget-lad
turns to the door, away from you.
He will be split apart and frayed
by sharp distress of shorn farewell;
but you must hear his footsteps fade
down a blown track where none can tell
what bend he took or say what morning
brings back the unlooked-for fugitive,
his arms about you without warning,
and no course left you but forgive.

Oh, girl, you have taken to your side
one as unresting as torn flame,
not of your people, who abide,
but of some country with no name
which rules by shadow of its laws,
flung far yet round him from of old,
till he is fretful for no cause
and leaves you, with his love half told,
to tread burnt roads of sand and gravel
or roads not rational which thrust
where only those would choose to travel
whose thoughts are grittier thirst than dust.

The Wind at Your Door

To MARY GILMORE

My ancestor was called on to go out—
a medical man, and one such must by law
wait in attendance on the pampered knout
and lend his countenance to what he saw,
lest the pet, patting with too bared a claw,
be judged a clumsy pussy. Bitter and hard,
see, as I see him, in that jailhouse yard.

Or see my thought of him: though time may keep
elsewhere tradition or a portrait still,
I would not feel under his cloak of sleep
if beard there or smooth chin, just to fulfill
some canon of precision. Good or ill
his blood's my own; and scratching in his grave
could find me more than I might wish to have.

Let him then be much of the middle style
of height and colouring; let his hair be dark
and his eyes green; and for that slit, the smile
that seemed inhuman, have it cruel and stark,
but grant it could be too the ironic mark
of all caught in the system—who the most,
the doctor or the flesh twined round that post?

There was a high wind blowing on that day;
for one who would not watch, but looked aside,
said that when twice he turned it blew his way
splashes of blood and strips of human hide
shaken out from the lashes that were plied
by one right-handed, one left-handed tough,
sweating at this paid task, and skilled enough.

That wind blows to your door down all these years.
Have you not known it when some breath you drew
tasted of blood? Your comfort is in arrears
of just thanks to a savagery tamed in you
only as subtler fears may serve in lieu
of thong and noose—old savagery which has built
your world and laws out of the lives it spilt.

For what was jailyard widens and takes in
my country. Fifty paces of stamped earth
stretch; and grey walls retreat and grow so thin
that towns show through and clearings—new raw birth
which burst from handcuffs—and free hands go forth
to win tomorrow's harvest from a vast
ploughland—the fifty paces of that past.

But see it through a window barred across,
from cells this side, facing the outer gate
which shuts on freedom, opens on its loss
in a flat wall. Look left now through the grate
at buildings like more walls, roofed with grey slate
or hollowed in the thickness of laid stone
each side the court where the crowd stands this noon.

One there with the officials, thick of build,
not stout, say burly (so this obstinate man
ghosts in the eyes) is he whom enemies killed
(as I was taught) because the monopolist clan
found him a grit in their smooth-turning plan,
too loyally active on behalf of Bligh.
So he got lost; and history passed him by.

But now he buttons his long coat against
the biting gusts, or as a gesture of mind,
habitual; as if to keep him fenced
from stabs of slander sticking him from behind,
sped by the schemers never far to find
in faction, where approval from one source
damns in another clubroom as of course.

This man had Hunter's confidence, King's praise;
and settlers on the starving Hawkesbury banks
recalled through twilight drifting across their days
the doctor's fee of little more than thanks
so often; and how sent by their squeezed ranks
he put their case in London. I find I lack
the hateful paint to daub him wholly black.

Perhaps my life replies to his too much
through veiling generations dropped between.
My weakness here, resentments there, may touch
old motives and explain them, till I lean
to the forgiveness I must hope may clean
my own shortcomings; since no man can live
in his own sight if it will not forgive.

Certainly I must own him whether or not
it be my will. I was made understand
this much when once, marking a freehold lot,
my papers suddenly told me it was land
granted to Martin Mason. I felt his hand
heavily on my shoulder, and knew what coil
binds life to life through bodies, and soul to toil.

There, over to one corner, a bony group
of prisoner waits; and each shall be in turn
tied by his own arms in a human loop

about the post, with his back bared to learn
the price of seeking freedom. So they earn
three hundred rippling stripes apiece, as set
by the law's mathematics against the debt.

These are the Irish batch of Castle Hill,
rebels and mutineers, my countrymen
twice over: first, because of those to till
my birthplace first, hack roads, raise roofs; and then
because their older land time and again
enrolls me through my forbears; and I claim
as origin that threshold whence we came.

One sufferer had my surname, and thereto
"Maurice," which added up to history once;
an ignorant dolt, no doubt, for all that crew
was tenantry. The breed of clod and dunce
makes patriots and true men: could I announce
that Maurice as my kin I say aloud
I'd take his irons as heraldry, and be proud.

Maurice is at the post. Its music lulls,
one hundred lashes done. If backbone shows
then play the tune on buttocks! But feel his pulse;
that's what a doctor's for; and if it goes
lamely, then dose it with these purging blows—
which have not made him moan; though, writhing there,
"Let my neck be," he says, "and flog me fair."

One hundred lashes more, then rest the flail.
What says the doctor now? "This dog won't yelp;
he'll tire you out before you'll see him fail;
here's strength to spare; go on!" Ay, pound to pulp;
yet when you've done he'll walk without your help,
and knock down guards who'd carry him being bid,
and sing no song of where the pikes are hid.

It would be well if I could find, removed
through generations back—who knows how far?—
more than a surname's thickness as a proved
bridge with that man's foundations. I need some star
of courage from his firmament, a bar
against surrenders: faith. All trials are less
than rain-blacked wind tells of that old distress.

Yet I can live with Mason. What is told
and what my heart knows of his heart, can sort
much truth from falsehood, much there that I hold
good clearly or good clouded by report;
and for things bad, ill grows where ills resort:
they were bad times. None know what in his place
they might have done. I've my own faults to face.

Said the Don
from *Between Two Tides*

"Señor," said the Don, "here there is none forgets
Pizarro's pencil, sword-point, and a line
drawn in the sand. On the near side lay Castile,
the power of Castile and the king's order: Return;
but beyond, where Pizarro stood, that was Peru
where the king's writ did not run, nor indeed knowledge.
Anything was there: all the unshackled earth,
fighting and fortune for rapacious hands,
empires greater than Spain, death almost certainly . . .
And, señor, you were free to go if you would
to safety and ships waiting. Few chose otherwise.
Yet there were thirteen crossed that line and turned
their backs on the past that prodded them and on Spain,
which meant that past and doubtless debts and miseries,
unless it meant the gallows. And if they were
desperate men lured on by greed, lust, gold;
cruel men gripped by a chill thirst for bloodshed;
then there is credit omitted when the account
is told against greed and cruelty; something which is
with it all, of the greatness of striving. It is not enough
that life should be lived justly, death met quietly;
though that's nobility also. But man's essence
is not nobility, it is man, unrest,
a rushing of wind, distance: distance which is
in the heart as much as in worn shoes, a carpet
unrolled over the world as we unroll one
over these earthen tiles when there is music
and little Micaela dancing. Man is these things;
and life's like a wave breaking, not good or ill,
or right or wrong, but action and pressing forward;
a thing tested in the heart which hears and answers;
as when we have men, near-naked and ill armed,
thirteen, half starved, setting out to conquer kingdoms.

"So sailed they south three centuries back, where now
others sail north to attack the Manila ship—
never deny what's plain. So, Señor Captain,
you too will wait perhaps by rainy Gallo.
Spare there a thought for an amiable man,
the Governor of Tola—for one who has lived
the life of cities and the life of the camp,
and finds it better to round off his days
in a dying village on a lonely coast

where what is left of them is real and naked,
being mixed with folk who share sea, wind and soil,
rather than rot in Lima on a diet
of piety and pension; though it is true,
as my daughter says, these would be spiced with scandal
and she could buy new slippers every day.
And then—for what I would say is that one lives
as one chooses to live, even though choice is blind—
think of another choosing; think of Pizarro,
his sun-dried face, hollow belly and thin legs,
and the sword-arm he'd have given for you men,
your ship, your cannon—fretting there on Gallo
in rain, heat, starvation, agony of mind.
Every hour holds its choice. We do the choosing;
but events present the straws. The ends are hidden;
who knows the short from the long? And when we are older
all straws are much of a length. I have chosen Tola.
Pizarro chose Peru. That youngster there
might have the world or nothing. And Micaela,
herself a straw, for God help any man's daughter,
might, Señor Captain, blow away in the wind."

Conflict

Ho, traveller on the barren roof
of this high country, had you ears
stroked by some quickening from old years,
beyond proving or need of proof;
then might you start at clash of hoof—
where with locked horns the hills engage
and primal warfares wage.

Conflict of shaggy rams of stone . . .
Savage great ridges, jarring, test
strength upon strength, crest reared at crest,
spur jolting spur's flint forehead-bone;
and these gaunt profiles are upthrown
knitted and twined against the murk
where olden seethings lurk.

For thus advances and takes toll
struggle inaugurate on that day
when gods unbuckled for the fray
at the first opening of the scroll
in the dawn of the world; thus did they roll—
thigh to bare thigh—and tear and thrust
mid earth's all-fertile dust.

Fought for the new toys barely made:
sea and cool air and souls of men—
whence this unquiet that again
raids and is met with counter-raid;
while you, lone traveller, undelayed,
click shoe to pebble on that fringe
where sky and earth impinge.

Go your way: why should you look or heed
who inherit also the strife? What breath
drawn by men but is aimed at death?—
arrows unequal to the need.
In your own contest, this, good speed!
Behind you the hooves charge: skulls break:
old cries shudder and wake.

Evening

Evening: it ripples cool to our held feet
like the bay's blacker crests, which idly crawl
along the stone seawall;
and as these, multitudinous, repeat
a moonlight-counterfeit,
so the new darkness crumpled against this town
bears in its every fold that brave deceit
which lets the world seem playtime, and our scars
(won in low skirmish) badges of pure renown.
This is the moment there returns to us
late memory of old bargains with such stars
as made the night-skies of man's infancy
fearful to walk in but miraculous.
Nor has that wonder gone: we square our debt
by sheer surrender to stark mystery,
staining its altars with spilt ecstasy
which in our fathers was a howl to the moon—
round lit doors, ransomed, we do not forget.

Long Since . . .

Long since I heard the muttered anger of the reef;
but it was far off even then, so far indeed
that an imagined murmur, like the ear's belief
and faith of the night, was mingled with a fuller knell
throbbing across the silence, and one could not tell
which sounds were of air stirring, which come at the mind's
    need.

And that was the old sea, alive beyond the calm
of those wide-reaching waters stifled in the lagoon—
alert, masterful waves summoning beach and palm
to be up and about and moving and ever upon quest
of new desires of the spirit, not sunk in a soft rest
only expectant of some drunkenness of the moon.

I knew it also for my own heart's call to me,
as baffling still as it would seem in the lost time
when it was loveliness on edge with melody,
elusive always and yet eternally to be sought
past any meaning of meaning or any thought of thought—
now wistfully heard again in even so dulled a clime.

I turned harshly and strode back to the native town,
watched by the wooden faces, the stolid Fijian eyes,
sought my thatched doorway, entered, mechanically sat down,
wondering what fate was on me or what weakness took toll
that thus I must go scurrying ratwise to my hole
lest some true self should claim me with imperious cries.

Rebirth

The fall of evening is the rebirth of knowing:

it is then the body looks up and is not alone;
for an old thought mingled with a newer thought
swells, breaks the dam and sets the whole tide flowing.

The tropic light over the sugarcane
was weary daylong; and the eyes only sought
to escape its colour, running from tuft to tuft;

but with evening a lost eagerness we regain
and watch how yellow of sunset will impress
its strength upon native green, how the green, rebuffed,

climbs helter-skelter to palm-tops, where they stoop,
weighed under feather-branches, their headdress.
All day though body walked upright, mind lay numb;

but as in the cool the gathering shadows group
so now some energies return from straying.
Back to our startled universe they come

and have zest for listening, seeing and marking down—
but yonder a song and a ukelele playing:
island airs sing in the heart its bitter truth. . . .

It is easier to let vague longings possess their own,
stretch and relax, though almost we knew some urge
to take up again the dropped threads of our youth.

Side Street

Back from the paved way this night is met
by the sea's lost children. A lamp's rivulet
streams over a brown body, a red sash;
for who walks here walks as a rainbow-splash
upon a curtain of jet.

Flowers in stiff hair; broad teeth, white-gleaming; black eyes,
smooth but still savage, caught in a molten flash;
the oiled skins; the rapt singing; the soft tongue:
be these remembered until memory dies!
And though I have known these people near their true core
in further, untroubled villages hid among
remote, rain-shattering hills where their lives make
no count of the years passing, I think of them more
here, pressed against a new meaning, a strange mode
unparalleled in the old path they forsake.

For here their steel must sharpen on harsh files
(race grinding race) to cleave now a fresh road;
else they shall tread the sunlight some few miles,
then, singing even with last bitter breah,
go decked in paper garlands down to death.

Fusion of bloods, submergence of past things,
eclipse, survival—it's tomorrow's care!
Dark Loma behind her lattice flicks the strings
and the tune steps out light-footed upon the air.

This Between Us . . .

Sleep at Lovo, old chief or warrior,
once my companion days and nights together,
you in your mound, the long grass over you,
I lying above the grass beside you.
You did not chide my nearness, neither by day
my comings and goings and more impatient waiting—
stamping up and down knee-deep among weeds,
beating the damp clay into a path at your head—
nor yet by night my lesser sleep than yours
where there we lay, the two of us, under the hills,
Nasorolevu behind us, the great lonely
weight of the night—empty between the hills—
over us, and Lovo stream at our feet
rattling, bubbling, boiling as it does now
in your deaf ears and my own ears remembering.

Nameless forgotten chief, I came
so long after you through that gash in the range,
Tagi-na-sola (meaning the-stranger-weeps,
met by this pass as enemy) that my climbing
that sideling track between bared teeth of boulders—
not fenced as once with spears but difficult still—
was to a place which enough years have changed
from just what ground you walked on who lie in it now
to surface that forgets and is other ground.
There I could reach all things that those years hoard
but found nothing your thought might share with mine.
And so your blood-splash lifetime, your eating of men,
your rites and loves . . . were of air only, lost,
not to be entered into or understood
or lit from within. Yet there is this between us:
that your world which is gone, and my world going,
are your darkness—the passing of what was—
and mine blotting tomorrow's windowpane—
the passing of what is. Then comes the stranger.

What mast on the sea? what sail? what smoke in the sky?
Shouts from the beach! Let the young men go down.
The sun we knew sinks drowning beyond Yasawa.

The Blue Thought of the Hills

Set down your load; it is vain,
all that your heart wills.
The hills have a high disdain—
you must never hope to attain
to the blue thought of the hills,
which marches beyond the thirst
of the dragging miles, leads on
where the last ridge beckons the first
with a promise of secrets nursed
in the far years gone.

For the hills have learnt so much
from the sky and the wide air,
their wisdom is not for the touch
of all-brief lives that clutch
at a fleeting share.
Although your way might aspire
from the peak to the further peak,
vision and blue retire;
beyond even desire
they are still to seek.

Edge

Knife's edge, moon's edge, water's edge,
graze the throat of the formed shape
that sense fills where shape vanishes:
air at the ground limit of steel,
the thin disc in the moon's curve,
land gliding out of no land.

The new image, the freed thought,
are carved from that inert bulk
where the known ends and the unknown
is cut down before it—at the mind's edge,
the knife-edge at the throat of darkness.

The Face of the Waters

Once again the scurry of feet—those myriads
crossing the black granite; and again
laughter cruelly in pursuit; and then
the twang like a harpstring or the spring of a trap,
and the swerve on the polished surface: the soft little pads
sidling and skidding and avoiding; but soon caught up
in the hand of laughter and put back . . .

There is no release from the rack
of darkness for the unformed shape,
the unexisting thought
stretched half-and-half
in the shadow of beginning and that denser black
under the imminence of huge pylons—
the deeper nought;
but neither is there anything to escape,
or to laugh,
or to twang that string which is not a string but silence
plucked at the heart of silence.

Nor can there be a floor to the bottomless;
except in so far as conjecture must arrive,
lungs cracking, at the depth of its dive;
where downward further is further distress
with no change in it; as if a mile and an inch
are equally squeezed into a pinch,
and retreating limits of cold mind
frozen, smoothed, defined.

Out of the tension of silence (the twanged string);
from the agony of not being (that terrible laughter
tortured by darkness); out of it all
once again the tentative migration; once again
a universe on the edge of being born:
feet running fearfully out of nothing
at the core of nothing:
colour, light, life, fearfully
becoming eyes and understanding: sound becoming ears . . .

For eternity is not space reaching
on without end to it; not time without end to it,
nor infinity working round in a circle;
but a placeless dot enclosing nothing,
the pre-time pinpoint of impossible beginning,
enclosed by nothing, not even by emptiness—
impossible: so wholly at odds with possibilities

that, always emergent and wrestling and interlinking
they shatter it and return to it, are all of it and part of it.
It is your hand stretched out to touch your neighbour's,
and feet running through the dark, directionless like darkness.

Worlds that were spun adrift re-enter
that intolerable centre;
indeed the widest-looping comet
never departed from it;
it alone exists.
And though, opposing it, there persists
the enormous structure of forces, laws,
as background for other coming and going,
that's but a pattern, a phase, no pause,
of ever-being-erected, ever-growing
ideas unphysically alternative
to nothing, which is the quick. You may say hills live,
or life's the imperfect aspect of a flowing
that sorts itself as hills; much as thoughts wind
selectively through mind.

The egg-shell collapses
in the first of the eternal instant;
all is what it was before.
Yet is that eternal instant
the pinpoint bursting into reality,
the possibilities and perhapses,
the feet scurrying on the floor.
It is the suspense also
with which the outward thrust
holds the inward surrender—
the stresses in the shell before it buckles under:
the struggle to magpie-morning and all life's clamour and lust;
the part breaking through the whole;
light and the clear day and so simple a goal.

Essay on Memory

Rain in my ears: impatiently there raps
at a sealed door the fury of chill drops—
knuckles bared of the flesh come rattling on
vaults that conceal a sorrier skeleton
huddled, unhearing, in a dark so deep
that this clear summons ruffles not calm sleep.

It is the hand of Memory come scratching
on the tomb of carrion buried from mankind—
forgotten by all except this body-snatching
walker of old night and times dropped from mind,
who knows where the slain rots and seeks it yet;
for Memory does not fail though men forget,
but pokes a ghost-finger into all our pies
and jabs out the dead meat, a grim Jack Horner,
mocking the mild dream, half guess, half lies,
of History babbling from his chimney-corner.

Memory is not that picture tacked on thought
among the show-girls and prize-ribbon rams,
wherein is last week's yesterday to be sought;
lens-twisted and fading, and yet somehow caught
in the known gesture, almost at speaking terms;
nor is it the sky-old story which in stone
within baked saurian footmarks prints its own,
as if the mud might soften and recollect
almost our lean beginnings and project
against the background of these days some far
horrible firmament, or show a star
choking with cloud whereunder, oozed from slime,
slow forms are dragging—half-way back through time;
nor is it composite mind whose cells are men
and whose dour genius grafts great stone on stone
by torch-flare lit on torch-flare—till it seems
that the tall topwork of new cornice gleams
in the glow of ancient lore, and sits firm-stayed
in masonry that hands long cold once laid.

Something of all this . . . but Memory peers
from the brown mottled ruin, shrieks and gibbers
among the fallen fragments of lost years,
lurks by the lichened archway, frights the neighbours
when a wind shrills about that older house
on which these days have quarried and made levies.
For Memory is the wind's voice in the crevice,

a wild song through those stones and in the boughs
of trees fast-dug in flint-chips of the novice;
it is the count of hooves for ever dinned
in the ears of the world by the hard-ridden wind;
and more than these and more than headlong haste
of events galloping through widening waste
into the cumulative past—to keep
galloping on with never pause nor sleep—
it is the past itself, the dead time's will
poisoning today's pulse and potent still;
it is the ruled heart's heritage, mortmain;
darkness it is and talons of the rain.

And under earth, so varied and so golden
telling must halt, lie jars which life's old trouble
brimmed gaily, which have felt that wine embolden
hopes that looked out on many a morning olden.
And were they dupes of the dawn, then, seeing double,
since all are smashed, the false clay like the noble,
knaves and brave men all gone, and dainty wenches?
Not, surely, while the grape yet spurts one bubble,
though vessels crack and are pushed down from their benches.
And these that there lie shattered, and their nights,
rapturous, and their days, or meek as prayer,
or polished like hard brass by glinting lights,
fell, each, before some fumbling hour, their slayer.
Now is the spread stain of their deaths long vanished
and the wine froths again and never gayer,
though theirs is all soaked up, dank earth replenished,
so it might seem the book closed, the tale finished;
yet are they loot of Memory, who comes
unrecognised from rifling those bleak tombs. . . .
Stranger at the door, like doom, disaster,
no man can bar you out, this house's master.

.   .   .   .

In our own garments left to face the drear
whinings of winter, stripped of gauds and gear
save what is patently our due and worn
by rights inherent, cold indeed were morn,
naked were noon. No comfort could we claim
except from that one wavering inward flame
unquenched through change and time, which though it
    wrought
in intricate iron the twisted chain of thought,
link by link stretching, vagrantly designed,
back past first hammerings of conscious mind,

is yet so fine, for all its intense white core,
stretched fingers freeze which were but chilled before.

(Strange miracle of self, mysterious, lit
no man knows how nor whence uprises it!
Lamp by lamp flickers out; this flame burns on
here—yet remotely here—and ever alone,
freezing and powerless, too, for each isled spark
were little avail against the encroaching dark
and life would perish on its pavement-flags
but that we clasp about us cast-off rags
and robes of dead kings. . . .)

                                 Rain over the world:
one handspan counts a million splashes hurled
minute by tireless minute; yet these are
random and wayward only, scattering far.
Denser, outnumbering the raindrop prisms,
there's a dumb deluge driven across night's chasms,
hard in upon us, unresisted, beating
our lives to patterns imposed past all defeating
by our poor wills; we are storm-carried, storm-shed,
battered by streaming multitudes of these dead.

They are about us on all sides: the dust
is restless; the bruised tongues of trodden weeds
speak with harsh voices, menace; grass-blades thrust
at parrying air that mirrors bygone deeds;
and who might think the unquiet is, at most,
wistful backgazing of the unbodied host,
homesick for life, who tread some screened-off path
of supernatural being beyond death,
let him once clutch at his own arms, so trussed
in thongs of old inheritance they can
but move in those accustomed tasks of man
allotted, limited, by the flesh they wear
ancestrally; he'll find an answer there,
fragile for sure, yet tougher than a ghost.

Indeed, we are the substance of their thought
which starves in air, can balance on no mystic
knife-edge of abstract being, twixt nought and nought,
so kneads itself in this inert, this plastic
material of our lives. But reckoning so,
farther and farther back, bared long-ago
which spores in shafts of time and mushroom-swells
through midnight-centuries, sees all things else
not as existence, but as forms worked over

in one huge bulk ere each is lost for ever,
not as reality but its escape
in impress after impress of pure shape,
and so dissolves the world. Now only appear
re-shuffling motion and the turn of the year:
all is become sheer action which perceives
bright leaves themselves as rustling of the leaves,
the bird's flight as the bird. This, heart denies
eternally; and Memory, too, replies—
links up the many flights upon one thread
of keen-eyed bird too busy to be dead
between flights done; for Memory stays the hour
and behind flower-growth is even the flower.
And we ourselves are Memory, and retain
so much of those gone, the little death can gain
is found a cheat of the senses; change and birth
convulsive writhings of autophagous earth.

. . . .

Argument is the blade-bright window-pane
which shears off cleanly the slant sheaf of rain,
and in the room heart's dream and life's desire
are radiance and curled, unfolding fire.
Here thought may ponder in peace or work at will
or take down book from shelf and read his fill;
but though among men's assets he bides long
always his ears are tuned on that same song
of rain outside; for that's the force he knew
which drenched his hands that battled it, breaking through,
while yet he was homeless in the world, unsafe,
wandering in mindless marshes the wind's waif,
and had not learned to build up words and fix
a house for himself in speech's bonded bricks.
Hearing it he remembers: though large walls
shelter him now, hold out the rain, rain falls.

And ever the untaught earth, comrade of yore,
out there under the dark and dripping leaves,
although its slave-bent back, laid bare, receives
whip-stripes of rain, possesses yet that more,
wisdom and fullness, which thought has not known,
never can reach. For earth, stooped labourer,
treading the furrow of seasons, early astir
and late abed from heavy fields, wild sown,
has wind and sun for sure realities,
endures this lash, too, as a thing plain-shown,
simple as flooded rivers, tumbling seas,

gaunt hills across the sky. . . . These are earth's own;
but thought has only sounds and shadows thrown
by hollow powers, obscure immensities,
upon the screen called living. And the good, solid
meat that earth munches, truth, is proved invalid;
thought is unfed—and even thought has grown
a trifle impatient of philosophies. . . .

And mourns, like Memory, old simplicities,
other truth yet, as stark as in years younger
trod the wet clay—till this plain truth of hunger
cries: "Time to rouse! Put by the reading-glass
which showed up print so clearly, a jagged mass
of black rocks in a dangerous foam of white,
showed more than sight could know, but not like sight,
split into jutting patches the blunt sense
and took more note of blots than eloquence.
Time now to trust our eyes, which if they find
less than the glass, less than contents the mind,
have yet their own sure knowledge of shape and fact
not as things purely are, but as they act.
And well to go among men, see how they do
the will of the past and bend their backs thereto,
the past that guides them, rules them, flogs—and flings
a despot's largesse, treasure of spoiled kings.
See how they walk between a day and a day,
command the future, and the past obey,
their present only a footing on some height
that fronts new dawn for ever, dazed with light;
see how their knowledge, between night and night,
asks, but not answers, whither winds the way."

.   .   .   .

If, as may seem, fair future spreads unfurrowed
beneath new morning and there writhes and wheels,
a sun-blind sea all silverly tomorrowed,
ruffled by promise and uncut by keels,
and, Dampiers of this dawn, we pull the prow
off-wind and pay out sheet, none tells us now
what bides our choice or if we drown or starve;
and even if the luck holds and we carve
new coasts on gaping latitudes, who traces
the scarless wake of an adventurer, lost,
sows wheat, finds gold, where we found desert places,
gashes with screws wide lanes where, lone, we crossed?

This hour, a gulp in the long throat of the past,
swallows what once was future, but soon spent;
this hour is a touch of hands, an accident
of instants meeting in unechoing vast:
it is a rail that bursts before the flourish
of black manes and time's haste; it fails our need—
now must decision be brief, must jump or perish
under the feet and fury of stampede.
And to this difficult present will succeed
what present, to be lost as this is lost?
for any decision may fall undermost,
and no hand counts the grandsons of its deed.
Foresight is but a bargain that we make,
which, even should life keep it, death will break.

. . . .

Who sees this time all edged about with wars
like tiny points of fire along the rim,
stretching to suns then sinking back to stars,
must hold heart-close his love to speak for him
and be his challenge to those rigorous teeth
that devour all, the answer of his faith—
which is towards the green-burst of new spring,
leaf-revelry and flower-strewn roistering,
life-joy and the dear miracle of increase.
Yet who stares forward through the shimmer of peace,
noon-heavy over valleys soaked in health,
and, baulked of sight beyond this burgeoning wealth,
finds only tremor-tapestry, hung haze,
will watch, adread, for the first beaconing blaze.
Or if the only smokes that, serpentine,
encoil the land be stubble-fires that twine
ribbons of incense round a harvest-feast,
still must one fear be troublous, one at least—
a vision of changed scene wherein smokes, black,
crawl venomous from a Gorgon chimney-stack,
with, deep below, all foreign to our ken,
strange engines and strange customs and strange men!
Well might our senses shudder when flesh hears
the coming Unseen, the spectre-march of years;
for though a man face fortunes horror-haunted,
gruesome with prophecies, and grin undaunted,
shall he bear blame from the accusing eyes
of legions grey with agony? bear their cries
sinking in floods of fire he dreams not of

and has condemned them to in very love?
Well may he see his children, such a one,
and groan doubt-drunkenly: "What have I done?"

Rain in the clean sun falling—riches of rain
wash out the dusty fear, the air's dull stain;
ay, Memory is a shower of gilded darts
which pins today's delight on our healed hearts,
or, in our hands, is mintage of bright faith:
shame on us to be beggared by a wraith!
Now, till this trove be gone, the last coin sped,
doubt were a glum ingratitude to the dead.
How should we hold us from wild enterprise,
who use the limbs of the past and its quick eyes
and are eternally in debt to those
who stung into the earth-dawn's turgid throes
urge of keen life? We'll crash the trestles down
that barricade clear laughter, take the town
on a burst of shouting that through fissures rent
cascades its fervid glee, magnificent.
We'll slit gloom's gullet, oracling defeat,
and crack great barrels of song in open street,
free for the drinking. We'll make fabulous
this world, in honour of them who gave it us,
not just the Nelsons, Newtons, of our race,
the Phillips grounding at a landing-place
continent-wide, but all whom violence of mind,
violence of action, gave such singleness
that if they did but grow, ambitionless
except to live in the sun, they served their kind
with that straight growth of will which bears for seed
zest to create; which, grasping at blind air,
graves flowers from veriest nothing and makes fair
all that we have. Theirs was that splendid greed,
hewer of men and vineyards, nation-maker,
destroyer of hate and weakness, tyrant-breaker,
whose slow attrition, whetstone of advance,
grinds laws, arts, customs, from steel circumstance.

Then knot this hour's activity as a rope
in strength of climbing hands; for still our hope
best clings to shoulders swarming—from the mouth,
black-gaping, of loss and failure; all we know
is this jerked ladder of change whereby men go
with gasping struggle, vigour of movement—up!
Wherefore all good is effort, and all truth
encounter and overcoming. . . .

                          We whose scope
clasps the tremendous leagues of summer-south,
thunder-oppressive with curbed energies,
least of all folk need question our day's worth
or think its turmoil twitchings of spent earth.
Here noon above burnt, bony ridges hung
nerve-tense, is strident with an unheard tongue,
pregnant with daring and with destinies;
and the mist-floating islands and raw seas
nigh us and those strained ranks of shores far-swelling
knit us with fortunes idle the foretelling.
And though we plan and make, for we would keep
won soil a little beyond the ruptured sleep
of bursting tomorrows gonged upon our ears,
it is little to hold this land star-counted years
or even to-night yield it; much that fever
pounds along resolute limbs its scorching river—
doings, upheavals—much that skies, bow-drawn,
are tautened by red-eyed but still tireless dawn....

Whatever the task, it lies in front: we must
build upward though we guess not to what skies,
and though the eruptive Babels that we thrust
vital in air will fritter back to dust;
else we betray the lamp behind our eyes,
the quickening in our veins, both held in trust
since long before the scumming of the germ
upon first seas. We will serve out our term:
not yet the impetus flags whose course began
when at the blank mouth of our stinking lair
we saw night's infinite curtain shake with grey,
and so went forth determined to be Man,
standing at last erect, and watched new day
wrap back the dark and strip the valley bare.

So, should our best work fail us, walls we planned
stifle in years blown over fine like sand,
or life itself reach gulfs and lorn extremes—
even some crag of ending—where bled dreams
kite in the wind weightless and the past
unclaws our very world, lets go at last,
but still remains, being Memory, one live link
of gone with all-to-come, and from the brink
peers out beyond; then, launched above that steep,
venture shall cant bold wings and with their sweep
splinter such clogging silence as they met
in older abyss where time slept stirless yet.

Entreaty

Summer come soon and turn the sickness from my house,
which from sour early darkness, damp wind, spiteful rain,
took shelter beside our fire, and through these months has lain
like a tame cat on the beds or crept up like a mouse,

or stood at doorways like a stranger's unwanted dog,
mangy and treacherous—ill comrade to be found
at play with children . . . So the comfortless time goes round;
and evening coughs cold air and dawn is phlegmed with fog.

Until it seems we must be utterly dispossessed,
unless on the world's shoulders that swing with the poles
    and dip
summer come cantering south to crack the sun, his whip,
about the lean hindquarters of my yelping, unpleasant guest.

Envy

Envy goes groping for the kisses
others have had of your mouth's red;
gropes in morass, and thereby misses
these, flowerlike, which have sprung instead—

these which are ageless and not vexed
by ancient jealousy, old grime,
but span this instant and the next,
trembling upon the edge of time,

hawks hung in the wind above that verge
where all falls bottomless and is nought,
whence the tomorrows shall emerge
which yet are cloudy and unwrought.

Poised at time's focus on strong wings,
like birds turned sharply into the gust,
your kisses have linked me to wise things
saner than envy or distrust:

Space for this moment is not more
than a swollen raindrop, which could burst
here at my lips and spill its store
of riches on my clamouring thirst;

and Now, holding its breath, reveals
how each new summer like saved wine
treasures old summers, and conceals
springs yet ungathered, and all mine.

So when I clasp you here I keep
all that dead lovers have desired,
waken their bodies from long sleep
and their dreams, changeless and untired.

Held thus, you become drawn breath of any
who have been loved—once named, once known;
and the brief lives of that white many
you hand on, deathless and your own.

There is only this embrace at last
anywhere: others touched you once,
but I touch all the present and past
and the wide sky's uncounted suns.

Bog and Candle

I

At the end of life paralysis or those creeping teeth,
the crab at lung or liver or the rat in the brain,
and flesh become limp rag, and sense tap of a cane—
if you would pray, brother, pray for a clean death.

For when the work you chip from age-hard earth must pause,
faced with the dark, unfinished, where day gave love and jest,
day and that earth in you shall pit you to their test
of struggle in old bog against the tug of claws.

II

What need had such a one for light at the night's rim?
Yet in the air of evening till the medley of sound—
children and birds and traffic—settled in the profound
meditation of earth, it was the blind man's whim

to set at his wide window the warm gift of flame
and put a match to wick for sight not like his own—
for his blank eyes could pierce that darkness all have known,
the thought: "What use the light, or to play out the game?",

yet could disperse also the fog of that queer code
which exalts pain as evidence of some aim or end
finer than strength it tortures, so sees pain as friend,
good in itself and guiding to great ultimate good.

Then he would touch the walls of the cold place where he sat
but know the world as wider, since here, beside his hand,
this flame could reach out, out, did touch but understand. . . .
Life in a man's body perhaps rayed out like that.

So it is body's business and its inborn doom
past will, past hope, past reason and all courage of heart,
still to resist among the roof-beams ripped apart
the putting-out of the candle in the blind man's room.

1918–1941

Not those patient men who knocked and were unheeded
where ignorance impeded like a flat panel swung
before the tower-stair to the dark mind of the young:
another moved beside them on the dais, at the desk—
War in a square cap, gowned and grotesque.

This was the master whose tongue did the talking;
then time became a chalking-off of dates upon the wall—
for no lad chose a calling who heard instead a call,
and just beyond a boy's years (so the lesson ran)
the one work waited fitting for a man.

None grew so tiptoe as to see the plain road, yonder,
at the hour's edge dip under to the leagues of calm before.
It was odd to break step and shamble from the door,
to plough the broad peace, and be older, and learn pride
from the day's task met and the morrow still defied.

Distant the guns are, and no wind veering
has brought them into hearing, nor yet in these lands
do they bawl between hills as between a pair of hands;
but there's what we were bred to . . . and strange it is then
to be lifting our sons up to watch the marching men.

Tattered the bewilderment I pull across my shoulders,
and shamed before beholders in this torn shirt,
like a slave to my shoes I wander unalert,
with eyes but no thought in them to mark the way I tread
and a thought without eyes that runs lost in my head.

Drift

Beware of rivers in the sun
that stay because they go.
What if the watcher by the stream
should drop into a dream.
and drown the life that he lets run
in just that drift and flow?

Become the stump upon the bank
above time's calm no-haste
which swallows much as water does
what even now it was,
a man might never learn what sank
the while his hours ran waste.

Then choose the churn of waves that chide
square headlands and taut ships,
or lakes where some upended peak
dredges the truths men seek.
Have pang of thought or pulse of tide
bring blood back to the lips.

As Between Neighbours . . .

Be close in your corner; for the thing not said
is a wise thing, worthy the grey, wise head.
Surely the silent man saving every word
has right coin for living in his tight-held hoard.

The grave word spoken is soon proved wrong,
and the gay word's a feather that's afloat in a song;
and he who is hollow sees life as a jest,
and laughter is the sign of him; silence is best.

Chain your laughter, neighbour, put a lock on your tongue:
that the old should be merry is offensive to the young.
The young man has forgotten, though we remember, toys—
with the world in his pocket like a marble in a boy's.

This Mutch
from *Roadside*

Having said that all the gums have not been cut
and dry sticks break beneath them; and having said
the grass is good this year, but shows a rut
developing here and there and looking red

along worn sides of hills; that as I walked
kicking up dust and powdered dung of sheep,
a hare came loping towards me, saw me, baulked,
crouched—then lost his nerve and fled with a leap;

that magpies gossiped above me on big boughs;
that tanks are three parts full though hard earth bakes;
that there are sheep, of course, a few dry cows,
not many rabbits, and I stirred no snakes;

having said this much I know and regret my loss,
whose eye falls short of my love for just this land,
too turned within for the small flower in the moss
and birds my father all but brought to his hand.

Verities

Out of history, beyond
reasoning thought, began
this cave's watch on the bond
kept between dog and man.

Man, though his hand's work
has a mind's aim, shall knock
his head, raised in the dark,
still on his roof's rock;

and still, though light may flood
his eyes each dawn, they clog
with needs and the greeds of blood
in flesh he shares with dog.

While dog, his brain in his nose
for fight or forage, a blend
of earth with life that it grows,
keeps fast this faith in his friend.

And the grey, hanging shelf,
that fellowship's third, looks on
as if it were time itself,
patient, older than stone

in which, like a chiselled truth,
changeless, the years engrave
a dog at a cave's mouth,
the dog's man in the cave.

Vision
from *Insight*

Though mind will shut out sight—
not too unkindly—
that one given the light
may yet walk blindly

not seeing at all
beyond his moment's need
raised like a blank wall
to part dream from deed,

with eyes held in a scope
safe from such daring
as peers out past hope
or strays, wayfaring;

the converse, nevertheless,
hardly applies:
scenes in the mind press
unchecked on the eyes.

From far times, far places,
from childhood, the past,
suddenly the old faces
rush in like a blast.

In the middle of business, thought,
or reading a book,
the thing watched comes all to nought
wherever you look;

and just for a leaping flash
a creek where the boy swam,
dried up by years that are ash,
floods the whole room.

Tocsin

And should that singing in your ears
be scythe-stone on the scythe,
cleaver and sickle, sword and shears,
have taken still their tithe
from green or yellow of the yield
and never scaled with rust
while harvest fluttered or there thrust
one stalk up from the field.

And you, alone here in your house,
believed you had in call
better company than the mouse
gnawing behind the wall,
not having learnt how walls fold in
narrowly where you dwell
until your self becomes your cell,
cut off from friends and kin.

Mostly, grey fellow, if you spared
a pause to think it through,
you saw the dark that must be dared
as no way meant for you,
nothing that need concern you much
with work or play on hand;
but there's a shadow where you stand
and at your wrist a touch.

No, it's no more than that a page
like one you turned on youth
flicks in your fingers now; and age
must read a further truth
hidden there in some word that gives
years yet or just an hour,
but suddenly shall speak with power
its cold imperatives.

What follows is for night to teach;
meanwhile this loudness bids
live hands and brain grasp all in reach
and eyes not shut their lids
on anything of earth that's found
intenser for threat's tone
shrilling, like locust-summer's own
which breaks off in mid-sound.

Southmost Twelve

Now at the year's midnight turned towards dawn,
the stroke of the southmost twelve deep in your ears,
you must not count upon the swing of the stars
to bring you back to sunrise. Light withdrawn
could sink past all renewal if logic gropes
at truth beyond astronomy's telescopes.

For that the sun rose every dawn of the world
from waves or crags or desert and rose to east
leaves all things possible still, this thing not least;
a western sun tomorrow in the uncurled
petals of morning. And though natural law
be urged against the argument there's no flaw.

Nor do I speak of miracle but what's plain
of any so-called law traced out in dust
by man's or nature's fingers: that it just
records things measured such as list of the moon
derelict on time's drift, or takes a glance
at temporary truth afloat on chance;

and nowhere says day certainly shall break
or the shocked sky, unprooted and flung hence,
would flare and fuse all that was order once
and yet not flout the mindless law, but make
its wheels the wrecker. Let light come or not,
it is time we struck a peace with our own thought. . . .

Meant thus: peace went which in a cruder age
bull's-blood, or honey mixed with wine and spilt,
ensured for skin-clad hinds who held men's guilt
called winter on them; but one might assuage
research that freezes reason and thaw both
with warmth in wisdom, near-half of all truth.

Myself, I never liked logic's rope, the theme
that step should tie on step. Why, as to that,
your first blind leap at premise can fall as flat
as mine where stones to tread on fail mid-stream;
and no man lives by logic or could suppose
there's logic in the fact that live he does.

But the cold cause-and-effect of mass and force,
of harnessed action under a shackled sky,
the powerlessness of will, I still deny,

who cross the road at choice or hold my course
and tell the gong of the clock that bangs this beat
not rope, and better than engine, leads my feet.

Creature of instinct, I share still the faith
of beast and bird, and call intelligence
knowledge of what I touch—what's bared to sense
as real itself, real in what lies beneath—
and doubt not of tomorrow opening where
the twang of this vibration thins in air.

Strata

This comfortable rock
of all our origins,
the immemorial clock
whereunder time begins,
stratum by stratum ticks
the seconds of earth's age
where birth and burial mix
their broth of heritage.

For what cools here has fed
bone of your body and bone
of life's whole structure, spread—
layer on layer like stone—
by hunger, animal needs
and pulse of will that brought
savagery of the breeds
up raw crags to thought.

But setting that aside,
so much of living falls
within the pacified
rock of erected walls
that it is easy enough
to rot and stay content
with a synthetic stuff,
a sapless nutriment.

So that I count this gift
priceless: that I have been
never so far adrift
from cliff, creek, ravine
and red gravel of the ridge
that from my youth on
I could not find some ledge
neighbourly to the sun.

A lean place and a waste
for profit; but one could
know in a world of haste
that deep down what withstood
the street's load was that starved
rock-mass to which one clung
inwardly, where, wind-carved,
it woke leaf-shadowed, bird-sung.

Glad World

I

The fakir upon his bed of nails
is happier than is thought.
Toughness of hide can blunt more ills
than could be dodged or fought:
the lesson is well taught.

And happiness, pivoted elate
on peace of mind, health, sleep,
food, kindred, good support like that,
knows too where wounds could creep
or suddenly sink deep.

II

Toss out the broken chairs!
Thus we progress;
and still the new methods and wares
concern us less
than the old needs and laughters, the whole affair's
untidiness.

Efficiency would complete
the set tasks row by row,
ends tied and neat.
Living is not done so;
its tramplings cross, circle, repeat—
in a glad world to know.

Everywhere—good to find—
is work in the rough.
Life picks up, leaves behind
thoughts broken off,
unfinished efforts of mind . . .
Death will be tidy enough.

III

I use this life to live in; I need eight more
for learning and ambition and to explore
where necessary haste
went by so fast

that there was only a vision, never proved,
of wider living: trees opening as one moved
showed it; and it was cut
by trees that shut.

Knowledge was like a leak—for hands to stop
since all the ocean's beyond it. One salt drop
only, is safe to drink;
lest the mind sink.

And action, earlier, climbing the hill's crest
with back to the east, saw roads run south and west
which would be lost henceforth
if one turned north.

But with wind blowing about him what's for a man
except press on towards breakfast while he can?
This hunger the gods give,
this once to live.

750 copies of *Of Some Country*
have been printed in Waverly type
by the Printing Division of The University of Texas
Design & typography by Kim Taylor
1963